WAS THE CROSS ENOUGH?

OR DID JESUS DIE TWICE?

DAVID ALSOBROOK

First Printing May 1984
100,000 copies

The publication of this book was made possible by
the freewill love gifts of God's people.

Abbreviations in this book mean:
NEB—The New English Bible
NASB—The New American Standard Bible
Fenton—The Holy Bible in Modern English
    translated by Ferrar Fenton
NIV—The New International Version
Lamsa—The Holy Bible from Ancient Eastern
    Manuscripts
Ampl.—The Amplified Bible

All pronouns in reference to deity are capitalized
without regard to varying styles of different
versions.

Unless otherwise noted all scripture quotes are
from the King James Version.

Designed and produced by Custom Graphics, Tulsa, Oklahoma

Contents

David Alsobrook Ministries
P.O. Box 2676
Paducah, Kentucky 42002

Preface

The sweet water of the Word is being poisoned by the bitter error of Satan's deceit. Wild gourds of vain philosophy are poisoning the pot of God's prophets (2 Kings 4:38-44).

It is our prayer this book will be an instrument of blessing in your life and in the lives you influence.

Together we can cast the tree of Calvary into the waters of Marah (Exodus 15:25) and the meal of sound teaching into the poisoned pot. Through the rightly-divided Word, the bitter waters will become sweet again and the pot of God's truth will be wholesome once more.

"It is the glory of God to conceal a thing, but the glory of kings is to search a thing out" (Proverbs 25:2, *Ampl.*).

Beware of the Leaven

A fairly recent abberration (delusion or deviation) of the simple atonement truth is now making wide circles (although it began almost fifty years ago through one pastor's lessons). I first heard the message of *Jesus suffering in hell* in the tender year of 1971. Barely two years old in the Lord and eager for in-depth teaching, I attended a seminar taught by a tremendous man of God. He expounded at length on the subject to my complete amazement and joy. My! what new and profound truths I learned that night! I was glad I had carefully recorded his remarks alongside the various references in my Bible. They would come in useful, I thought.

Yesterday I studied those references again —thirteen years later—looking over my notes in the margins of the well-worn Bible. The twenty-second Psalm brought memories of that night long ago and the preacher's voice I heard once more. The notes and memories brought no joy to me this time. Solemnity and sobriety filled my soul. What an awesome responsibility we teachers have to equally balance a straight line through the Word of God! I realized anew how in God's watchful care I had unknowingly drunk a deadly thing. In His grace it had not hurt me.

My messy notes alongside the verses read, "the spirit separated from His Father," "large demons ready to pounce," and so forth. How pink indeed were the rosy glasses through which I first looked.

In 1972 I studied all the books voicing this teaching. The well-sounding phrases slipped through my mouth in bits and pieces when preaching. Sometimes something deep inside said, "That's wrong!", but my teenage mind refused to listen to my toddler spirit.

One evening that year a dear old pentecostal preacher approached me at the close of a service. I had not given this elder much credit for Bible knowledge before, but had always welcomed his attendance and joy. He told me I needed to "pray through about Jesus in hell" as he put it.

That following day I took his kind advice and "prayed through." For the next several months I studied the atonement day and night and prayed much more. So many things were shown me by the revelation of the Holy Spirit. Thereafter I corrected the "bits and pieces" of error I had formerly preached whenever visiting churches where I had voiced the words of man.

For years since I have preached the faith I once destroyed (however minimally), teaching instead the great Bible truths of redemption by the blood. In 1976 I devoted only four short pages of my book *The Precious Blood* in refute of the doctrine that *Jesus suffered in gehenna* during the intervening three days between the crucifixion and the resurrection. At that time this error was not as widely known and circulated as it since has become.

My concern has steadily increased over this teaching in the Body of Christ to the point that I must now write a much longer reproof. The basis of this concern is the fact that "a little leaven leavens the whole lump" (Galatians 5:9).

Acceptance of the doctrine of *Jesus dying spiritually* has led to distortions of many Bible truths (i.e., the character of Christ, the sovereignty of God, the ability of Satan, etc.). Paul's remark about leaven to the Galatians concerned their acceptance of the Mosaic ritual. To many this would not be a cause for great alarm, yet the apostle rightly observed, "Christ is become of no effect unto you, whosoever of you are justified by the law; ye are fallen from grace" (Galatians 5:4).

A little leaven *(Jesus becoming a sinner on the cross)* may eventually "leaven the whole lump" of what was once a tremendous move of God. The unfortunate reality may be the fulfillment of Peter's prophecy: "...there shall be false teachers among you, who privily shall bring in damnable heresies, EVEN DENYING THE LORD THAT BOUGHT THEM, and bring upon themselves swift destruction... And through coveteousness shall they with feigned words make merchandise of you..." (2 Peter 2:1,3).

Across the land other preachers are likewise hearing the voice of God. It is time that every teacher in the Body of Christ evaluate in prayer and study the message he teaches in the light of James' warning; "Do not be eager, my brethren, for many among you to become teachers; for you know that WE TEACHERS SHALL UNDERGO SEVERER JUDGMENT" (James 3:1, *Weymouth*).

Much damage is done to the integrity of God's Word when one reads into the Bible what it does not say. May every minister of the Word heed this wise admonition:

"Every word of God is pure: He is a shield unto them that put their trust in Him. *Add thou not unto His words*, lest He reprove thee, and *thou be found a liar"* (Proverbs 30:5-6).

8

The Three Views of the Cross

God's altar of sacrifice, the cross, can be perceived in only three ways: naturally, religiously, and spiritually. The *natural eye* views the cross as utter, absurd foolishness. As Paul told the Corinthians: "For the preaching of the cross is to them that perish foolishness...But the natural man receiveth not the things of the Spirit of God: for they are foolishness unto him..." (1 Corinthians 1:18; 2:14).

The second way the cross is understood is with the *religious mind*. There are many Christians who view the cross as only partially appeasing God's hatred for sin. While giving lip service to the validity of Christ shedding His precious blood, the religious mind insists the cross is not enough and something more must be added to seal man's salvation.

To those in Galatia who were accepting "another gospel" from the persuasion of the Judaizers, Paul declared: "O foolish Galatians, who hath bewitched you, that ye should not obey the truth, before whose eyes Jesus Christ hath been evidently set forth, crucified among you..." (Galatians 3:1). It can be safely said that every perversion of redemptive truth throughout the Church's history has consistently minimized the singular importance of the blood.

The third way the cross can be seen is by the *enlightened mind*. This is an individual to whom the Holy Spirit has revealed the all-sufficiency of the man Christ Jesus dying upon a Roman stake. Any addition to His work is an abberration from the simple truth declared in His Word. "...without shedding of blood is no remission...Blotting out the handwriting of ordinances that was against us, which was contrary to us, and took it out of the way, nailing it to His cross; And having spoiled principalities and powers, He made a shew of them openly, triumphing over them in it" (Hebrews 9:22, Colossians 2:14-15). The enlightened believer sees Jesus bowing His head declaring "IT IS FINISHED" and does not misconstrue it as meaning "to be continued." The Apostle Paul gloried in the sacrifice of Jesus on Golgotha's hill: "But God forbid that I should glory, save in the cross of our Lord Jesus Christ..." (Galatians 6:14).

Where Did Jesus Bear Our Sin?

It would be scriptural to consider the man Christ Jesus as a tripartite (or three-fold) being: spirit, soul, and body. His body was created and fashioned by the Holy Spirit in a virgin's womb. His soul was a perfect emotional and intellectual life force. His spirit was the immutable Logos of God eternally established. This Logos (or Word) was made (or robed) with flesh and dwelt (or tabernacled) among man. So John introduces Jesus in the first chapter of his gospel (verse 14).

Some teach that Jesus Christ became sin on the cross in the realm of His spirit being. In order to do this, they say, He ceased to be deity on the tree quoting the Psalm of the Cross in support of their view. "But I am a worm, and no man; a reproach of men and despised of the people" (Psalm 22:6). One evangelist told me, "This is where Jesus ceased to be divine. He said, 'I am a worm and not a man' meaning that Jesus was not the sinless one anymore."

It is plain to see these teachers interpret

Christ's prophecy of Himself on the cross through David to mean He was no longer divine in His spirit being. The "worm" in this verse is the Hebrew word *tola*. The *tola*, quite surprisingly, is the crimson-colored grub worm in Palestine which was used centuries ago for making red dye! So much was this worm associated with scarlet dye that *tola* was actually translated THIRTY-ONE TIMES in the King James Version as "scarlet" rather than "crimson-grub" or "worm." How beautiful is the prophetic claim: "I AM A *TOLA*..." Jesus fulfilled the role of the *tola* in shedding His precious blood on the cross!

Another truth apparent from Psalm 22:6 is the fact the word "man" used by David in this verse is *ish* and was used in his day of comparing great men to ordinary men. In effect Christ was saying, "I am the lowest of the people and no great man" (see *Dake's Annotated Reference Bible* for further application). This seems to be the proper interpretation when studied, as it should be, with the rest of the verse: "But I am a worm, and no man; *a reproach of men and despised of the people.*" Certainly this statement of the Messiah being a worm and no great man was intended by David to mean that scorners (not God) regarded Him as such. To imply otherwise requires a far stretch of the imagination.

The simple truth is *Christ has never ceased to be divine at any time in His eternal existence.* Peter emphasizes this fact when he teaches Christ was righteous while suffering for sins. "For Christ also hath once suffered for sins, the just (righteous) for the unjust (unrighteous), that He might bring us to God, being put to death in the flesh, but quickened by the Spirit" (1 Peter 3:18).

Isaiah also illuminates this truth in his often-quoted prophecy of the Messiah's sufferings. During the same time in which He would bear iniquities our Lord is termed "My righteous servant." "...by His knowledge shall My righteous servant justify many, for He shall bear their iniquities" (Isaiah 53:11). Jesus' sacrifice was acceptable to God because He was righteous while bearing our iniquities on the cross.

The spiritual nature of Jesus remained unchanged on the cross. Paul taught that GOD WAS IN CHRIST DURING THE EVENT OF RECONCILIATION! "To wit, that God was in Christ, reconciling the world unto Himself..." (2 Corinthians 5:19). This appears only two verses before the often-quoted (but misinterpreted) statement that God "made Him to be sin for us, who knew no sin; that we might be made the righteousness of God in Him" (2 Corinthians 5:21). God made Jesus sin

13

(or "a sin-offering" according to many authorities) in His body on the tree. The author of Hebrews concurs: "...we are sanctified through the offering of *the body* of Jesus Christ" (Hebrews 10:10). Peter confirms Christ "bare our sins *in His own body* on the tree, that we being dead to sins should live unto righteousness" (1 Peter 2:24). The Word of God specifically says that Jesus "abolished *in His flesh* the enmity" (Ephesians 3:15).

It is dangerous to teach Jesus became sin in His spirit because it undoes His eternal deity. As we will study in the next chapter, the Bible teaches the spirit of our Savior went *immediately* to His holy Father in heaven the moment He died.

Another point in the defense of the sinlessness of His spirit is the point that the Word which created the worlds was the spiritual nature of Jesus. This WORD (Logos) also upholds all the creation He made "by the WORD of His power" (Hebrews 1:3). It is obvious that had Jesus' spiritual nature bore our sin, the worlds would have dissolved because the Word made flesh not only made them but also upheld them. The Spirit of Christ was the Word and the Word did not die because the Word is God and God cannot die or be made into sin. "...and the Word was God" (John 1:1).

The popular reasoning that Jesus had to die spiritually because man was spiritually dead sounds logical enough to the natural mind. Reason is good when it is Bible logic. Man, it is true, was spiritually dead in sins and in trespasses (Ephesians 2:1). Jesus did not have to die spiritually to correct this problem, however, because His blood is activated in the spiritual realm. In fact, had Jesus died spiritually (and this was impossible) He could not have redeemed man since He would need a redeemer Himself. Biblical reasoning states that Jesus had to shed His blood because man was spiritually dead. Every objection to this statement will be clearly answered as we continue in our study.

Let us go back to Isaiah's great atonement chapter to answer one objection and in the process see how precious the blood of Christ truly is to our redemption. "Yet it pleased the LORD to bruise Him; He hath put Him to grief: when Thou shalt make His soul an offering for sin, He shall see His seed, He shall prolong His days, and the pleasure of the LORD shall prosper in His hand" (Isaiah 53:10). The phrase "shalt make His soul an offering for sin" is often quoted in teachings promoting the spiritual death of Jesus.

A practice invaluable to a Bible teacher is to research key words in their original languages. There are many helpful study aids (lexicons, Hebrew/Greek dictionaries, etc.) widely available on the market. The word *soul* in Isaiah 53:10 is the Hebrew word *nephesh* and is best defined as *the natural life force* in its Old Testament usage. Literally Isaiah says, "Thou shalt make His *nephesh* an offering for sin."

Quite interesting is the use of *nephesh* in Leviticus 17:11 where Moses used it thus: "For the life (nephesh) of the flesh is in the blood: and I have given it to you upon the altar to make an atonement for your souls (nephesh): for it is the blood that maketh an atonement for the soul (nephesh)." Meditating on these two verses I suddenly saw an amazing truth. (Remember that Isaiah said that God would make the *nephesh* of Christ for a sin-offering and that Moses said the *nephesh* is in the blood.)

Please notice something:

*Isaiah said "Thou shalt make His 'nephesh' an offering for sin..."

*Moses said "the 'nephesh' of the flesh is in the blood..."

1. Because the 'nephesh' of Christ was made a sin-offering, and

2. Because the 'nephesh' is in the blood, we can deduce

3. "Thou shalt make HIS BLOOD an offering for sin!!!"

Rather than teaching Jesus died spiritually making His inner man an offering for sin in this often-used verse from Isaiah 53, the original language teaches that God made Christ's blood the offering for our sins!

The Scriptures make it abundantly clear to the honest-hearted that Jesus was made "a worm" *(tola)* WHEN HE SHED HIS BLOOD FOR US. (It was a rope dyed with the *tola* which Rahab hung in her window as a true token of her coming deliverance.) Our deliverance is based in the blood of Christ. My earnest prayer for the Body of Christ in recent years is may we never allow the enemy to minimize **the importance of the blood of Christ**. Those in heaven realize its fundamental importance: "And they sung a new song, saying, Thou art worthy to take the book, and to open the seals thereof: for Thou wast slain, and hast *redeemed us to God by Thy blood* out of every kindred, and tongue, and people, and nation..." (Revelation 5:9). The messenger told John concerning a group of others he saw clothed with white robes, "These are they which came out of great tribulation, and have washed their robes, and *made them white in the blood* of the Lamb" (Revelation 7:14).

Where Did Jesus Go?

Let us establish that at His death the *spirit* of Jesus went UP to His Father. the *soul* of Jesus went DOWN into the realm of sheol/hades for three days and three nights. (We are considering the term "soul" now as it is used predominately in the New Testament of the mind, will, and emotions comprising the natural personality.) The *body* of Jesus was laid IN a rich man's tomb.

It is true there is no separation of the spirit and soul in all other deaths. The death of the sinless Savior was, of course, unique and full of purpose. A possibility of the spirit separating from the soul is taught in Hebrews 4:12. "For the Word of God is living and active and sharper than any two-edged sword, and piercing as far as *the division of soul and spirit*, of both joint and marrow, and able to judge the thoughts and intentions of the heart" *(NASB)*. Please allow me to propose the possibility that there occurred a division of the soul and spirit at the moment of His death. The Word teaches that Jesus was in two places at one time during the 72-hour interval of the cross and empty tomb. I am not asking you to accept this possibility at face value, but to consider it under the careful scrutiny of Scripture.

1. HIS SPIRIT WENT UP

"When Jesus therefore had received the vinegar, He said, It is finished: and He bowed His head, and GAVE UP THE GHOST" (John 19:30). The King James Version translates the Greek word *pneuma* as "ghost" in many places. The modern word is "spirit." All textual authorities in all Gospel accounts of the death of Jesus agree unanimously that the spirit of Jesus went UP at death. "And when Jesus had cried with a loud voice, He said, 'Father, into Thy hands I commend (commit) my spirit: and having said thus, he GAVE UP THE GHOST" (Luke 23:46). "Jesus when he had cried again with a loud voice, YIELDED UP THE GHOST" (Matthew 27:50). "And Jesus cried with a loud voice, and GAVE UP THE GHOST" (Mark 15:37).

In denying these phrases denote a literal location, some have said our Lord "gave up" in a figurative sense, like one who gives up under the pressure of an unsolved problem. Luke's account, however, informs us it does denote a literal location since Jesus committed His spirit INTO THE FATHER'S HANDS before yielding up the ghost. The Father's hands are in the same location as the Father. Jesus often referred to the "Father in heaven" and the "heavenly Father."

Approximately eighteen hours before He gave UP the spirit He *"lifted up His eyes to heaven, and said, Father..."* (John 17:1).

Furthermore, He told His disciples several times during His last discourse with them that He was leaving this world in order to go to the Father. A five-chapter section of John's Gospel (chpts. 13, 14, 15, 16, and 17) contains the important teachings of Jesus to His disciples during the last supper. These chapters provide us an intimate inside look at the dialogue which filled that large, upstairs room. Notice these particular statements out of the mouth of Christ concerning His destination:

> "...and greater works than these shall he do; because I GO UNTO MY FATHER" (14:12).

> "...If ye loved Me, ye would rejoice, because I said, I GO UNTO THE FATHER... (14:28).

> "But now I go my way TO HIM THAT SENT ME..." (16:5).

> "...ye shall see Me, because I GO TO THE FATHER" (16:16).

> "I came forth FROM THE FATHER, and am come into the world: again, I leave the world, and GO TO THE FATHER" (16:28).

> "And now I am no more in the world, but these are in the world, and I AM COME

TO THEE. HOLY FATHER, Keep through thine own name those whom Thou hast given Me, that they may be one, as we are...AND NOW I COME TO THEE" (17:11, 13).

In a vain attempt to subvert the clear statement from the dying lips of Jesus: "Father, into Thy hands I commend My spirit..." (Luke 23:46), one minister went so far as to say that Jesus was speaking *to Satan who was now His father!* This blasphemy can be easily reproved by noting the closing prayer of the sacred Passover meeting in John 17:11, 13 quoted above. Notice that Christ referred to His Father as "holy:" "Holy Father...now I come to Thee." He concluded His high priestly prayer by addressing God as "O *righteous* Father..." (verse 25). It was to this same Person our Lord dismissed His spirit being.

It is likewise said that Jesus could not have physically died had He not spiritually died. According to the Word of God death occurs when the spirit leaves the body. "For as the body without the spirit is dead, so faith without works is dead also" (James 2:26). When Jesus gave up the spirit to His Father the physical body died.

Another way some teachers get around the clear statements of the Gospels, concerning the spirit of Christ being committed to His Father at death, is by their insistent teaching that God

21

rejected the spirit of the Savior (since it supposedly had been made sinful) and turned Him over to Satan for further punishment in the fires of hell.

Acts 2:23-28, another misinterpreted passage, actually teaches that the spirit of our Lord always saw His Lord (the Father) before His face because He (Christ) was on His right hand that He should not be moved. Therefore, His heart rejoiced and His tongue was glad during the same period in which His physical body lay in the tomb. The *spirit* of Christ knew the Father would not leave His *soul* in hell (sheol/hades) nor permit His *body* to see corruption. Yes, the *spirit* of Christ said to the Father, "Thou hast made known to Me the ways of life" *before* His soul came up from the bowels of the earth and His lifeless body was quickened.

Having just paraphrased Acts 2:23-28 we will now carefully read and study this often-misunderstood portion of Scripture. Note please, that Peter was quoting Psalm 16 and applying David's statement to the Lord Jesus. It is obvious to all that these verses speak of the interval between the crucifixion and resurrection.

> "Him, being delivered by the determinate counsel and foreknowledge of God, ye have taken, and by wicked hands have crucified and slain: Whom God hath raised up,

having loosed the pains of death: because it was not possible that He should be holden of it. For David speaketh concerning Him, I foresaw the Lord always before My face; for He is on My right hand, that I should not be moved: therefore did My heart rejoice, and My tongue was glad; moreover also My flesh shall rest in hope: because Thou wilt not leave My soul in hell, neither wilt Thou suffer Thine Holy One to see corruption. Thou hast made known to Me the ways of life; Thou shalt make Me full of joy with Thy countenance."

The phrase "...because Thou wilt not leave My soul in hell..." is widely used by those who teach that "Jesus died spiritually," as the common saying goes. The Greek word translated "hell" in this passage is *hades*, and according to Bible dictionaries, means, "the realm of the dead; the Greek counterpart of the Hebrew *sheol.*"

Since the ascension, when Jesus ascended up on high, the only ones left in hades are the lost, who occupy that part of hades known as "gehenna"—the fires of hell. Before the ascension, however, paradise was just as much a part of the realm of the dead as was gehenna.

Paradise was occupied with all those who "died in faith, not having received the promises..." (Hebrews 11:13). The blood of animal sacrifices could not actually take away the sins of the old covenant people (see Hebrews 10:4), but, could only temporarily cover them until Jesus came and made redemption for the sins under the first covenant (see Hebrews 9:15). When faithful Israelites died they did not go to heaven, but went instead to Abraham's bosom which was a place of comfort. Abraham himself was not in heaven, but in sheol/hades still waiting entrance into the city God had built for him and for us (see Hebrews 11:14-16).

The incident told by Jesus in Luke 16:19-31 illustrates this point. Lazarus was carried by the angels into Abraham's bosom at death, whereas the certain rich man was in torment (pain) in hell. There was a great gulf fixed between the two areas, but it is certain they were both in the same locale (otherwise they would not be able to converse).

We read again and again in the Old Testament of individuals who died and were "gathered unto their fathers." It is my conviction this phrase refers to the after life. I could go into many illustrations from the Old Testament to establish this point, but it would detract us from our main consideration. Suffice it to say that this fact gives us special insight into the meaning of John 8:56 where Jesus said, "Your father Abraham rejoiced to see My day: and he saw it, and was glad." God permitted Abraham to look up through the bowels of the earth and witness the Incarnation. It made him glad knowing that God Himself had provided the Lamb of which he had prophesied in Genesis 22:8. Only a few more decades and Abraham would be ushered into the heavenly country he had left Ur of Chaldees to find so many centuries before!

Going back to Peter's sermon on the day of Pentecost, we affirm with him that the soul of Jesus was in hades during the three days and three nights (as we will study later under Point Two), however, not in the area of punishment (gehenna) but in the area of comfort (Abraham's bosom). Jesus promised the repentant thief: "Verily I say unto thee, Today shalt thou be with Me in paradise" (Luke 23:43). Not meaning that the thief would be accompanying the spirit of Jesus going to the Father, but that he would accompany Jesus' soul in its descent into the bowels of the earth (where paradise was at that time).

Now take a look with me at the rest of Peter's quotation from the sixteenth Psalm: "For David speaketh concerning Him, I foresaw the Lord always before My *face;* for He is on My *right hand,* that I should not be moved: therefore did My *heart* rejoice, and My *tongue* was glad..." These words are spoken by the pre-incarnate Word through the mouth of David and are to find their fulfillment during the same period when "...moreover also My flesh shall rest in hope: because Thou wilt not leave My soul in hell (hades), neither wilt Thou suffer Thine Holy One to see corruption..."

During the same period in which His body would rest in hope and not see corruption; during which His soul would not be abandoned in hades; the spirit of Jesus was in the Father's presence (I foresaw the Lord always). Notice: "...He (the Father) is on My right hand..." He did not say "will be" but "is." Rather than suffering torment, Christ said His "tongue was glad" in contrast to the rich man in hell who besought Abraham to send Lazarus and "cool my tongue" (Luke 16:24).

One may also surmise from Peter's quotation of Psalm 16 that the references to: face, right hand, heart, and tongue refer to the spirit being of Jesus whose body was resting in hope (of the resurrection). In like comparison to the rich man of Luke 15 who "died and was buried" where his physical eyes and his physical tongue were entombed with the rest of his body. Yet Jesus said "...in hell he lifted up his *eyes*..." and also quoted his request for Lazarus to "...dip the tip of his *finger* in water, and cool my *tongue;* for I am tormented in this flame" (Luke 16:24).

Christ's spirit was in the presence of God *after* the crucifixion and *before* the resurrection. His heart was rejoicing in the knowledge of God's wisdom. "Thou hast made known to Me the ways of life" Jesus said to His Father. This was before His soul left hades or His body was resurrected. (Note the verb structure: "...Thou *wilt not* leave My soul in hell, neither *wilt* Thou suffer Thine Holy One to see corruption. Thou *hast made known* to Me the ways of life...").

As you are aware, the believer's spirit has *eyes* that can be enlightened, *ears* that can hear the Holy Spirit's voice, and a *tongue* that can taste the goodness of the Lord (see Ephesians 1:18; Revelation 2:7; Psalm 19:10; 34:8).

In conclusion of Point One it is well established that the spirit of Christ, the divine LOGOS of all the ages, went immediately from the cross to heaven to rejoice in the Father's presence.

2. HIS SOUL WENT DOWN

"Then certain of the scribes and of the Pharisees answered, saying, Master, we would see a sign from thee. But He answered and said unto them, An evil and adulterous generation seeketh after a sign; and there shall no sign be given to it, but the sign of the prophet Jonas: For as Jonas was three days and three nights in the whale's belly; so shall the Son of man be three days and three nights in the heart of the earth" (Matthew 12:38-40).

In this passage Jesus draws a parallel

between Jonah's experience in the belly of the great fish and His own soon-to-come experience in the heart of the earth. Jonah spent three days and three nights in the fish's belly and the fish stayed submerged the whole time until it spat Jonah out on the dry land. It was not a "whale" in the literal sense (the KJV translators chose that word in some passages), but, a large fish specially prepared by God for this event (see Jonah 1:17). A whale is an air-breathing mammal. A fish "breathes" water and usually stays submerged. Jesus likened Jonah's 72-hour submersion to His upcoming baptism into death in the above text.

Christ's baptism (literally: immersion) would be "in the heart of the earth." This phrase denotes the bowels of this planet, or "the lower parts of the earth" into which Jesus descended (see Ephesians 4:9). It cannot refer solely to the rock-hewn tomb in which is His lifeless body was lain.

Furthermore, when the mother of James and John besought the Master to sit her two sons to the right and left in His future reign, He replied: "Ye know not what ye ask. Are ye able to drink of the cup that I shall drink of, and to be baptized with the baptism that I am baptized with? They say unto him, We are able. And He saith unto them, Ye shall drink indeed of My cup, and be baptized with the baptism that I am baptized with.." (Matthew 20:22-23).

Notice, our Lord tied "the cup" and "the baptism" together in His response to this ulterior inquiry. After much reflection on these two terms, I believe the former refers to "the cup of suffering" which Jesus drank at the hands of wicked men during the crucifixion, but that the latter speaks of his baptism (burial, immersion) into the earth. Notice the words of His supplication in the Garden of Gethsemane: "O My Father, if it be possible, let this cup pass from Me: nevertheless not as I will, but as Thou wilt...He went away again the second time and prayed, saying, O My Father, if this cup may not pass away from Me, except I drink it, Thy will be done" (Matthew 26:39, 42). He drank the cup on the cross. At death the cup of suffering was finished.

Today some are teaching the worst was yet to come; supposedly several passages in the Psalms concerning the suffering of His inner man were yet to be fulfilled. Usually emphasized is Psalm 86:12-13: "I will praise Thee, O Lord my God, with all my heart: and I will glorify Thy name for evermore. For great is Thy mercy toward me: and Thou hast delivered my soul from the lowest hell."

It must be understood, before commenting

on this Psalm, that not all David said was messianic. Nor is it all intended to be taken in a literal sense: "What ailed thee...ye mountains, that ye skipped like rams; and ye little hills, like lambs?" (Psalm 114:5-6). This is but one example of the inspired imagery we read in the lovely poems of the Spirit. The sweet singers of Israel sometimes used figurative language for emphasis. Not a few commentators believe the same to be the case with Psalm 86:12-13. I differ with their valuable views at this point, however, and believe that David was expressing personal gratitude from eternal judgment which he knew he merited. I, too, can say, "For great is thy mercy toward me: and thou hast delivered my soul from the lowest hell." I was ready to take my life when Jesus snatched me from the fires of gehenna. In the eyes of God I was already condemned because I had not the Son (see John 3:18), and was likewise in a "pit wherein is no water" (Zechariah 9:11). By contrast today, I am positionally seated with Him now in heavenly places (see Ephesians 2:6).

Regardless of our personal views on Psalm 86:12-13, however, we should allow the Word of God where it specifically addresses the topic concerning Christ's fulfilling of the prophecies to be the direct answer itself. Shortly before He died, the Gospel of John tells us that this

Suffering Servant knew "that *all things were now accomplished*, that the scripture might be fulfilled" (John 19:28).

John's use of the term "scripture" in this verse includes ALL the sacred writings of the Law, the Psalms, and the Prophets. According to the plain statement of John, our Lord satisfied all the requirements in the Old Testament concerning His sin-sacrifice, BE-FORE He dismissed the spirit being into the Father's hands. Previously He had made it clear to His disciples that no man could take His life from Him, but, He would lay it down voluntarily of His own will (see John 10:17-18). As soon as He knew inside His innermost being that He had accomplished the task for which He was sent...HE LEFT! Rather than taxing all physical resources to the limit and dying as a man struggling to remain alive until the last possible moment, He freely dismissed His spirit from His body to the Father and so died (see James 2:26). Pilate, who knew firsthand the physical sufferings of Jesus, "...marvelled if He were already dead..." when Joseph of Arimathea asked for the lifeless body (see Mark 15:43-45).

At the moment of death, the spirit of Christ went at once into the presence of the Father, rejoicing in the accomplishment of the perfect sin offering. The soul of Jesus, along with that of the repentant thief (Luke 23:43), descended into the bowels of this planet where paradise was at that time located. At the ascension of Christ, paradise was moved as part of the "captives in His train" (Ephesians 4:7, *NIV)* and is now a part of "the third heaven" (see 2 Corinthians 12:2, 4).*

There is indeed no record anywhere in the New Testament of His sufferings extending beyond the cross. A few teach that Jesus did not suffer physically at all, but only emotionally and spiritually, basing their assumption on the fact that no Gospel tells us that He suffered any pain during His scourging and crucifixion. The writer of the letter to the Hebrews, however, speaks of His suffering as a temptation (or, trial) and a thing which He endured. "For since He Himself was tempted *in that which He has suffered*...who for the joy

*It is a personal conviction, subject to correction, that Christ also visited another compartment which First Peter 3:18-20; 4:6 describes in which the souls of those who drowned in the Flood were kept until they had the opportunity for Jesus to present the Gospel to them. According to Genesis 6:1, people already covered "the face of the earth" when Noah found favor in God's sight. The century plus that Noah preached righteousness was only to those in his vicinity. The ark builder did not travel abroad and warn of the impending judgment that would engulf the entire planet. Although all mankind was engrossed in awful sin, it does not follow biblical principle of warning prior to judgment, that millions one day looked up and saw rain for the first time and drowned without any forewarning to repent. Those who had heard Noah's preaching, on the other hand, were probably excepted from this mercy "prison" and went to gehenna upon death. It was not a second chance that Jesus gave, but a first chance to those who perished in ignorance.

that was set before Him *endured the cross...*"
(Hebrews 2:18; 12:1, *NASB).*

Concerning "the cup" which He was to
drink and "the baptism" with which He was to
be baptized, a popular slant is that Jesus
drank the awful cup of the sin nature (thus
becoming sin itself in His spirit being), and
was immersed into the fires of hell as all
sinners must be at death. Recall in this
passage (Matthew 20:22-23), however, that
Jesus told James and John that they both must
likewise "drink indeed of My cup, and be
baptized with the baptism that I am baptized
with..." If the above interpretation is correct
then Jesus was informing two of His close
followers that they, too, would become sin in
their spirit and suffer in hell for it! After all,
they were later to drink the same cup...

This popular teaching did not originate
with God. Jesus warned, "The man whose
teaching originates with himself *aims at his
own glory"* (John 7:18, *Weymouth).* The only
way to keep one's teaching pure is to seek only
the glory of God in all he or she teaches. "He
who aims at the glory of Him who sent him
teaches the truth, and there is no deception in
him" (remainder of the verse).

In water baptism there is a symbolic parallel to the baptism with which Jesus was
immersed. As the new believer is immersed

into the water he or she identifies with the descent of Christ into sheol. As the believer is raised up from the "watery grave" a parallel is drawn to the resurrection and ascension of Jesus. The old man, that was nailed to the cross with Jesus, is buried in the waters of baptism. The new man is raised up to walk in the newness of life. "Or don't you know that all of us who were baptized into Christ Jesus were baptized into HIS death? We were therefore buried with Him through baptism into death in order that, just as Christ was raised from the dead through the glory of the Father, we too may live a new life. If we have been united with Him in His death, we will certainly also be united with Him in His resurrection" (Romans 6:3-5, *NIV*).

One of the primary reasons Jesus descended into hell, according to this error, was to engage in war against Satan and defeat him at the moment Christ was born of the Holy Spirit in the pit. Flexing His spiritual muscles our Savior is said to have hit the lion in the mouth, knocking out his teeth. At that point, one brother told me, Jesus bound Satan hand and paw (sort of like modern westerns, I suppose), and grabbed the keys of hell and death from the adversary. He then walked over to the gates of the prison house of Satan and unlocked the gates of hell, allowing the captives held for centuries in gehenna to be freed. The more I hear "war-in-hell" stories, each differing slightly from the others, according to the whims of each speaker, the more I am convinced that only in America could such fiction be devised by minds raised on television and motion picture fantasy.

The error reveals a fundamental flaw in understanding redemption. The scriptural principle is not that "Jesus had to go to hell where He paid the price," but, that Jesus had to offer Himself "the righteous for the unrighteous" (1 Peter 3:18) that He might bring us to God, "...having been physically put to death, but SPIRITUALLY LIVING; in that condition He also went and preached to the spirits..." *(Fenton Translation).*

The Scripture teaches that Christ had to go to the cross where He had to pay the price for our sins. One of the words translated *sin* in the New Testament is the word for "debt—something that is owed." By studying the parable of the unforgiving servant in Matthew 18:23-25, it is clear Jesus meant the debt of ten thousand talents was owed "to a certain king" of which our Master likened "the kingdom of heaven." The lord, or king, turned the forgiven servant (who was in turn unforgiving of a fellow servant) "over to the tormentors..." Jesus concluded the parable with a plain statement: "So

35

likewise shall My heavenly Father do also unto you, if ye from your hearts forgive not every one his brother their trespasses." The "certain king" could be none other than "My heavenly Father." It is God against whom we have sinned (see Psalm 51:4) and to whom we must give an account (see Romans 14:12). We owed Satan nothing. (He could attack us due to our rebellion against God, leaving us open to his control.) Jesus went to the cross to give His holy life in exchange for Adam's sin. He paid the penalty of our transgressions against the Creator with the invaluable price of His costly blood.

"The physical blood of Jesus could not atone for man's sin because sin is a spiritual force," a well-meaning (but misguided) friend told me. I asked him to realize that he was quoting a statement he had heard many times and intreated him to consider 1 Peter 1:18-19 with me: "Forasmuch as ye know that ye were not redeemed with corruptible things, as silver and gold, from your vain conversation received by tradition from your fathers; But with the precious blood of Christ, as of a lamb without blemish and without spot." One of the meanings of the word "precious" in verse 19 is "rare" (as gold and silver are likewise rare metals in comparison to common ore). I pointed out to my friend that Jesus paid for the spiritual penalty of the spiritual force of sin with His rare kind of blood. (The blood of Jesus is a different type of blood than any ever offered to God before the cross. His blood is rare, unique, valuable, costly, and highly honorable according to one Greek dictionary of the word "precious." Although His blood was physical, it was without the stain of sin. His blood was completely pure and is activated in the spiritual realm by faith.)

This dear brother received in a flash the truth of God's Word. While meditating later upon this truth, a modern allegory was quickened in his spirit. When a person puts up bail money for an incarcerated friend, the money provides the release from the jail cell. After the money is put up the individual is not required to take the place of his friend and go to jail in his behalf.

Peter uses a similar analogy when employing the term "redeemed" in 1 Peter 1:18-19. This word was used in Peter's day in the slave market trade. Silver and gold were the medium of exchange used in redeeming physical slaves. Peter tells us we were not redeemed with silver and gold from our slave market, but with the costly blood of Christ. Thus, *the precious blood of Christ is the medium of exchange in the spiritual realm.* He offered Himself as a lamb without spot or defect to satisfy the demands for righteousness in the sight of God.

It's obvious from John 8:21 that Jesus didn't go to the place of torment when He left this earth, as those who "die in their sins" do...

> "Then said Jesus unto them, I go My way, and ye shall seek Me, *and shall die in your sins:* WHITHER I GO, YE CANNOT COME" John 8:21.

In addition to these truths, another error has been made concerning Satan's position in hell. As we will see in the next chapter He is not to hell what God is to heaven. That is, he is not and will not sit on a throne. Hell is not Satan's domain, but his prison. There is not one reference anywhere in Scripture (I have researched the entire Bible about this) which alludes to the common supposition that Satan regularly visits hell or that he has even been there once! He is not to be included with other angels who went after "strange flesh" and have been "reserved in everlasting chains under darkness" (Jude 6). When Peter tells us these angels were "cast down to hell" (2 Peter 2:4), he uses the Greek word *tartarus* for hell. *Tartarus* only appears this one time in the entire Greek New Testament and appears to be a holding tank for the "sons of God" in Genesis 6 who went in unto the "daughters of men." In this place they are "reserved for judgment" *(NEB)*.

Our adversary is roaming the earth seeking to deceive, if it were possible, the very elect.

Bible Answers
To Frequent Questions

In this chapter I will endeavor, by the grace of God, to answer questions which are often asked me by honest believers. Each of the following questions has been asked frequently during the past several years. Some questions are exact quotes from letters; others are compiled from memory. All accurately represent the various impressions left upon the minds of the hearers of this teaching.

Wasn't it necessary that Jesus engage in battle with Satan in hell in order to defeat the enemy on his own territory?

First of all, it is wrong to assume that hell is Satan's territory. Jesus said that hell was prepared *for* and not *by* the devil (Matthew 25:41). Hell was created by God for the devil's eternal abode in everlasting punishment. The devil, of course, would like us to think that he is in charge of this dreadful place. In all damnation no one else will suffer as great torment as he.

Secondly, an unbiblical concept dating back to Dante's *Inferno* places the adversary in authority in hell. According to medieval mythology the devil is to hell what God is to heaven. In this erroneous concept, he assigns various degrees of torment to hell's inhabitants. In contrary view, the psalmist taught that *God* would rain fire, brimstone, and an horrible tempest on the wicked (Psalm 11:6). Likewise it is clear Satan will be thrown into the lake of fire before any lost soul is hurled into it (compare Revelation 20:10, 15). This proves the devil will be undergoing eternal torment long before the first human is cast into the lake of fire.

The sensational "war-in-hell" stories are unscripturally based on these mythological inaccuracies. Literally dozens of these fictional battles in hell vary according to the particular whims of different preachers. Without misrepresentation of any kind, their concept of Satan's relationship with the infernal regions is totally inaccurate. When privately asking various teachers about these different points I am repeatedly told that God cannot make anything which is destructive. This reveals a clear misunderstanding of the foundational truth of "eternal judgment" (Hebrews 6:2). When Christ taught that we are not to fear them which can kill the body and after that have nothing more they can do, but to fear Him who has the power to destroy both soul and body in hell, He was definitely teaching us to fear God (see Matthew 10:28). (I speak of the reverential fear and awesome respect we are to give God.) The writer to the Hebrews affirms: "It is a fearful thing to fall into the hands of the living God" (10:31). Throughout the Old Testament God often judged the rebellious nation of Israel with famine, plague, war, captivity, etc.

Returning to the question of whether it was necessary for Jesus to engage Satan in direct conflict in hell (in order to defeat him on his own territory), we see that hell was never Satan's territory in the first place! Christ met and defeated the devil on his own territory to be sure, but that territory was located on earth, not hell, where Satan operates as the god of this world (see 2 Corinthians 4:4).

Christ did not dispute the tempter's claim to have all the kingdoms of this world under his domain (see Matthew 4:8-9). Paul speaks of "the prince of the power of the air" (Ephesians 2:2) and Peter tells us that our "adversary, the devil, as a roaring lion walketh about seeking whom he may devour" (1 Peter 5:8).

Furthermore, Satan's throne is not in hell at all, where he has yet to pay his first visit to the federal prison of the universe, but *on earth*. Jesus said to the church at Pergamum, "I

41

know where you live—*where Satan has his throne...*" (Revelation 2:13, *NIV*). Christ spoke those words to John near the end of the first century, proving *Satan makes this throne where it will accomplish the most evil: among the living.*

In conclusion Jesus most surely did defeat Satan on his own territory—and did so for years! Not once did Christ succumb to temptation. "I shall not talk much longer with you, for the prince of this world approaches. *He has no rights over Me;* but the world must be shown that *I love the Father, and do exactly as He commands;* so up, let us go forward!" (John 14:30-31, *NEB*). Dying on the cross was not due to a satanic mastery over Jesus (He never traded masters), but due to a perfect submission to the will of the Father. "...although He was a Son, He learned obedience from the things which He suffered; and being made fully equipped by sufferings, He became to all who obey Him a source of eternal salvation" (Hebrews 2:8-9, alternate rendering).

Didn't the Church begin in hell when Christ was born again in Satan's presence?

You are correct in implying this present error teaches Christ was born again in the pit of hell and thus became the first member of the Church. This was supposedly the way in which Jesus defeated Satan after He had suffered at the hands of Satan three days and three nights.

The opposite to this assertion is true. The Church did not begin in hell, but had its origination in heaven where all its files are kept (see Luke 10:20; Hebrews 12:23). The Founder claimed, "I came down from heaven..." (John 6:38) to "lay in Zion for a foundation a stone..." (Isaiah 28:16). The Church emerged on earth at Pentecost as recorded in Acts two. As the 120 waiting believers received the Holy Spirit they were baptized into one body and became the Body of Christ that day. One hundred and twenty bodies went up into the upper room; ONE BODY came down! (see 1 Corinthians 12:13; Ephesians 1:22-23).

When Christ said He would be lifted up on a pole as Moses lifted up the serpent in the wilderness, wasn't He saying He would take on Himself the serpent nature at Calvary?

Let's begin this answer with a look in the Amplified Bible at the verse: "And just as Moses lifted up the serpent in the desert [on a pole], so must—so it is necessary that—the Son of man be lifted up [on the cross]" (John 3:14). Jesus drew upon an event from Israel's past as a type He would fulfill for the salvation of mankind. In Numbers 21 we have recorded for us the experience of the fiery serpents who struck hundreds of murmuring Israelites. Many were dying under judgment.

Moses interceded for the people. "Then the LORD said to Moses, 'Make a fiery serpent, and set it on a standard; and it shall come about, that everyone who is bitten, when he looks at it, he shall live.' And Moses made a bronze serpent and set it on the standard; and it came about, that if a serpent bit any man, when he looked to the bronze serpent, he lived" (verses 8-9, *NASB*).

A fairly unknown fact is the Israelites associated healing with the pharoahic symbol of a serpent coiled around a rod. They had seen it four long centuries during Egyptian servitude. We see it today on ambulances, various medical associations, prescription labels and doctors' offices.

God had shown His healing power to Israel at least twice previously (on the night of the first Passover and at the waters of Marah). He had given them a redemptive name—Yahweh Rapha—to call upon for healing. Like us, the children of Israel were slow learners!

When God instructed Moses to construct a bronze serpent on a pole (so it would be high enough for all to see) He was, in essence, telling the people, "I, the LORD your God, am taking the place of the medical authorities in which you formerly trusted." As wounded Israelites looked upon the brazen serpent "attentively, expectantly, with a steady and absorbing gaze" *(Ampl.)* they were healed of snakebite and lived.

Jesus compared the wilderness event to His forthcoming crucifixion when He would likewise be lifted up on a Roman stake. Whoever placed their unswerving faith in Him would never perish (the next verse). It is clear Jesus meant the healing symbol would find its fulfillment in Him alone. When we look upon Him (whom we have pierced) we are healed of "snakebite" both spiritually (of sin) and physically (of sickness). Whoever looks upon Him will be radiant and will not be put to shame!

If the brazen serpent was meant to symbolize Satan, then God was telling the Israelites to look to Satan for healing! If the brazen serpent was meant to symbolize an object synonomous with medicine that they might release faith in an object to which their minds were adapted then we see it was God who healed the expectant Israelites.

The brazen serpent in the wilderness was not a symbol of Satan because God would never have His people look to the devil for anything! It was a *symbol of healing* upon which the people focused their gaze and were healed by Yahweh's power. From then on they would look to Him only for healing from all their diseases. He was replacing the symbol in which they formerly trusted.

By hanging on a tree as a condemned criminal Jesus appeared "in the *likeness* of sinful flesh" (Romans 8:3). He was not a sinner, but received a sinner's treatment as He died alongside two thieves. By dying in the guise of sinful man, Jesus was made a sin-offering for man! "For what the law was powerless to do in that it was weakened by our sinful nature, God did by sending His own Son in the likeness of sinful man to be a sin offering" (Romans 8:3, *NIV*).

When Jesus was "wounded for our transgressions" the "LORD laid upon Him the iniquity of us all" (Isaiah 53:5-6). Christ reconciled both Jews and Gentiles "unto God IN ONE BODY BY THE CROSS, having slain the enmity thereby" (Ephesians 2:16). The present error that Jesus took on the serpent nature, rather than the likeness of sinful flesh, makes the cross a means to an end. The Bible teaches it is the end itself; "...without shedding of blood is no remission" (Hebrews 9:22).

If sin is a spiritual force, how could a physical death sufficiently atone? Did not Jesus die spiritually to remedy man's spiritual condition?

46

The good-sounding statement that man was spiritually dead, therefore Jesus died spiritually, etc. is based on human logic rather than divine revelation. Let us see IF THE BIBLE SAYS the physical death of Jesus was sufficient to provide our salvation. Please read each of the verses given in several translations and pray for wisdom and understanding. We'll begin our survey with Colossians 1:21-22 in several versions for an example and quote the others in only one version for you to follow up on your own.

(KJV): "And you, that were sometime alienated and enemies in your mind by wicked works, yet now hath He reconciled IN THE BODY OF HIS FLESH THROUGH DEATH, to present you holy and unblameable and unreproveable in His sight;"

(NIV): "Once you were alienated from God and were enemies in your minds because of your evil behavior. but now He has reconciled you by Christ's PHYSICAL BODY through death to present you holy in His sight, without blemish and free from accusation—"

(Amplified): "And although you at one time were estranged and alienated from Him and of hostile attitude of mind in your wicked activities, Yet now has [Christ, the Messiah,] reconciled [you to God] IN THE BODY OF HIS FLESH through death, in order to present you holy and faultless and

irreproachable in His [the Father's] presence."

(NASB): "And although you were formerly alienated and hostile in mind, engaged in evil deeds, yet He has now reconciled you in HIS FLESHLY BODY through death, in order to present you before Him holy and blameless and beyond reproach—"

(NEB): "Formerly you were yourselves estranged from God; you were His enemies in heart and mind, and your deeds were evil. But now BY CHRIST'S DEATH IN HIS BODY OF FLESH AND BLOOD God has reconciled you to Himself, so that He may present you before Himself as dedicated men, without blemish and innocent in His sight."

(Fenton): "You, however, were once alienated and estranged, through your mind being addicted to the practice of vice; but now He has reconciled again, THROUGH THE DEATH OF HIS CORPOREAL BODY, to place you in the presence of Himself holy, blameless, and irreproachable:"

Other scriptures which emphasize the physical death of Jesus for the perfect sin-offering are:

(Hebrews 10:5, *Amplified):* "Hence, when He (Christ) entered into the world, He said, Sacrifices and offerings You have not desired, but *instead You have made ready a body for Me* [to offer]:"

48

(Hebrews 10:10, *NASB*): "By this will we have been sanctified *through the offering of the body of Jesus Christ once for all.*"

(Hebrews 10:19-20, *KJV*): "Having therefore, brethren, boldness to enter into the holiest by the blood of Jesus, By a new and living way, which He hath consecrated for us, through *the veil, that is to say, His flesh:*"

(1 Peter 4:11, *KJV*): "Forasmuch then as Christ *hath suffered for us in the flesh...*"

Some men say the physical death of Christ was not enough to make us right with God. The Bible says, "But now He has reconciled you by Christ's physical body through death, to present you holy in His sight" Colossians 1:22, *(NIV).* Some are interpreting the Bible in the light (?) of their redemption theories. We would do far better to interpret our redemption in light of the Scriptures.

The theory that the physical death of Jesus could not atone for sin because sin is a spiritual force undoes the purpose of the Incarnation. The great purpose of the Incarnation was that Christ could redeem men by His death on the cross and thereby defeat Satan: "Forasmuch then as the children are partakers of flesh and blood, He also Himself likewise took part of the same; that through death He might destroy him that had the power of death, that is, the devil" (Hebrews 2:14). The Word partook of blood and flesh (literal) that through

49

His physical death He could render Satan immobile.

If the reasoning of this new gospel were taken to its logical completion, one could do away with the Incarnation entirely, assuming it was necessary that Jesus die spiritually at the hands of Satan (compare Acts 2:23). Behind this doctrine is the spirit of antichrist which numbers of well-meaning young preachers are unknowingly giving heed to! The devil is very subtle in his disguise as an angel of light whereas he is only an angel of darkness. First John 4:3 teaches that the spirit of antichrist does not acknowledge the Incarnation. Many ministers give lip service to it, but turn around and deny the purpose for the Incarnation!

Isn't it true that Jesus never questioned the Father until the sin nature was poured upon Him at the cross and He cried, "My God, my God, why hast Thou forsaken Me?"

If we look at the commonly called "seven statements from the cross" we see the nature of God shining forth clearly in His final earthly hours. Jesus supposedly became sin itself in His inner being when He was hoisted in the air. In counselling with many people to forgive their debtors, I have noticed again and again it takes divine love filling the heart to do so. "Father forgive them for they know not what

50

they do" does not sound like a serpent's hiss to me!

In the midst of all the pain and suffering our Example said, "Woman, behold thy son" in reference to John and, "Son, behold thy mother" in reference to Mary. From that day forward John cared for Mary as he would his own mother. The godly concern manifested by Jesus for Mary's temporal and emotional needs brings tears to my eyes. How could this be Satan, whom we are mistakenly told was now His master, speaking from the cross? When I hear such things, I really get tears in my eyes for the spiritual well-being of the men who say such blasphemy, knowing they are snared by the words of their mouths and taken captive by the words of their lips.

As has been said before throughout this book, it is obvious that Jesus bore our sins in His body, through His physical death, paying for our sins with His special (one meaning of the word "precious") blood. Nor do the Scriptures teach that our Lord lost His sonship with the Father at any time. In fact, had He not been the Son when He died, He could not produce sons now: "For it became Him, for whom are all things, and by whom are all things, in bringing many sons unto glory, to make the captain of their salvation perfect (literally, fully equipped) through sufferings"

(Hebrews 2:10). His going to the cross is termed "an act of righteousness" by Paul (Romans 5:18).

"My God, my God, why hast Thou forsaken Me" is the first line of what is popularly termed "The Psalm of the Cross." Most scholars will tell you that Christ probably quoted the entire Psalm of which the Gospel writers recorded but the first line. This may be the case, however, I have come into a different understanding as the result of much research on the line preceding this quote. For years I wondered about the literal translation of "ELI, ELI, LEMANA, SHABAKTHNAI!" Have you ever pondered why it was left untranslated? If it was common Aramaic it would *not* have been printed in your Bible (the reason being that almost everything else Jesus said was probably in common Aramaic).

This took me on quite a search. I asked many pastors and teachers if they knew anything about it. Several said they thought Jesus was speaking in tongues as when He previously said "Ephatha" when praying for a deaf man. Boy, WAS I SURPRISED WHEN I FOUND OUT WHAT IT MEANT!! (You will be, too!)

"Eli, eli, lemana, shabakthani" (which is the most accurate spelling in English) is a literal utterance in an *uncommon* Aramaic dialect and this is what it means (get ready): *MY GOD, MY GOD, FOR THIS I WAS SPARED!!*

Jesus was spared from previous attempts on His life to fulfill His destiny on the cross. "For this purpose I came to this hour" (John 12:27, *NASB*). The Lamsa translation from *The Peshitta* which means "original," comes from the Aramaic, rather than the Greek manuscript. Note this translation in the two passages in which the "Eli, Eli..." statement is quoted:

> "And about the ninth hour, Jesus cried out with a loud voice and said, 'Eli, Eli, lemana shabakthani! My God, my God, for this I was spared!'" (Matthew 27:46, *Lamsa*).
>
> "And at the ninth hour, Jesus cried out with a loud voice, saying, Eli, Eli, lemana, shabakthani! which means, 'My God, my God, for this I was spared!'" (Mark 15:34, *Lamsa*).

The above translation agrees entirely with the theme of scripture: God will never forsake the righteous one who trusts in Him. John 16:32 makes it clear that Jesus expected the Father to be with Him throughout the entire ordeal of His soon coming execution: "Behold, the hour cometh, yea, is now come that ye (the disciples) shall be scattered, every man to his own, and shall leave Me alone: and yet I AM NOT ALONE, BECAUSE THE FATHER IS WITH ME." A few hours before it happened

Jesus told His disciples they would leave Him but said He would not be completely alone when they departed because the Father would remain with Jesus. Christ did not lie. Paul confirms that "God was in Christ" during the time of reconciliation and never tells us when He left Jesus because He never did.

Didn't drinking the full cup to the last of the bitter dregs mean that Jesus suffered three days and nights in hell fire to pay the full price?

Jesus drank the cup the Father gave Him to drink when He "taste(d) death for every man" (Hebrews 2:9). That this cup involved actual suffering in hell is an insupportable premise as IT WOULD NOT BE POSSIBLE FOR ONE PERSON to suffer in the short space of 72 hours the ETERNAL AGONY OF ONE LOST SOUL, let alone the whole race of mankind! Jesus is the world's Lamb which means He would have had to suffer all the torment of every person ever born for all eternity in three short days! After all, if this is what "the full price" means then that is exactly what had to have happened. But it didn't. As we have seen again and again this error presupposes wrongly and unbiblically, thinking out the things of God with the minds of men.

If drinking the cup meant suffering in hell, then Jesus told James and John they would have to suffer in hell, too. Please consider these words of Christ:

> "But Jesus answered and said, Ye know not what ye ask. ARE YOU ABLE TO DRINK OF THE CUP THAT I SHALL DRINK OF, and to be baptized with the baptism that I am baptized with? They say unto Him, We are able. And He saith unto them, YE SHALL DRINK INDEED OF MY CUP..." (Matthew 20:22-23).

The cup of which He spoke was the cup of suffering. James and John suffered for the sake of the gospel in the years that followed. Faced with the obvious fact, a dear lady scolded me anyway. "Well, I don't care what you show me in the Bible. My Jesus was willing to go to hell for my sins." (She claimed to be a "Word woman"!) Clearly our Lord Jesus would be willing to do anything for mankind, but going to hell would not have sufficed since *atonement could not be made there*. The type in the Old Testament was the Altar of Sacrifice in the Outer Court in which Gentiles could not enter. Gentiles speak figuratively (not literally) of the lost. We know the lost are in hell. Gehenna could never be an acceptable altar for a sin-offering in the sight of God.

A faulty understanding of the mechanics of

the sacrificial procedure is clearly shown by insisting that Jesus went to hell where the price was paid. The price was not, nay, could not be paid there. There is nothing redeeming or transforming about that place.

Jesus did not owe Satan anything for the redemption of mankind!

One of the great failings of modern theology in general is the enlarged, unbiblical view of Satan. This concept makes our God too small and our devil too big. Satan did not have to be paid a legal price for the redemption of men's souls. His ability to attack man and hold him under bondage was due to the sin debt man owed God and which he could never repay. A debt was OWED TO GOD and Jesus "was delivered for our offences, and raised again for our justification" (Romans 3:25).

It could be indelibly imprinted in our thoughts that ALL SIN OFFERINGS IN THE OLD COVENANT WERE ONLY OFFERED UNTO GOD! It was His justice which had been spurned and His laws which had been broken. It took His Son's spotless sin-offering on the cross to satisfy the demands of His righteousness. Jesus is our *goeleka*. This is a Hebrew word for "kinsman redeemer" which means "a relative who can pay his family's debt." Jesus became one of us when He took on flesh and blood. With that same blood He paid our debt toward God. The blood of Christ is the medium of exchange in the spiritual realm.

Corresponding to the Old Testament pattern, Jesus "offered Himself without spot to God" on the cross "the Altar of Sacrifice" and carried His blood into the heavenly Holy of Holies where He sprinkled that precious substance on the true Mercy-Seat accomplishing an eternal redemption for us!

When Paul states that God made Jesus to be sin for us, does he not mean that Jesus actually became sin on the cross, consequently at death Christ went where all sinners go at death?

We need to study 2 Corinthians 5:21 in more depth. This is the only place in the New Testament where we are told that Christ was "made sin for us." The NIV reads "God made Him who had no sin to be sin for us..." and marks the phrase "to be sin" with a footnote which reads *"a sin offering."* These scholars were correct in placing this footnote, knowing that Paul, a Hebrew of the Hebrews, was using a HEBRAISM. A *Hebraism* is a term which means an idiom or expression of speech used in a Jewish sense. The casual reader fails to notice this important fact which is why we are encouraged to "Study to shew thyself approved unto God a workman that needeth not to be ashamed, rightly dividing the word of truth" (2 Timothy 2:15).

The use of the Hebraism makes the verse read this way: "GOD MADE HIM WHO HAD NO SIN TO BE A SIN OFFERING FOR US..." In the Hebrew language of the Old Testament, one and the same word is used for both "sin" and "sin offering"—*chatta't*. In the Book of Leviticus this word is used dozens of times for *holy* sin offerings. The requirement set forth repeatedly in the levitical sacrificial laws (which Jesus perfectly fulfilled for us) was that the lamb be without spot or blemish (physically) to typify the Lamb of God (spiritually) when He was offered for us. In the old covenant the *chatta't* when used to mean "sin offering" was called "most holy" by God before, during, and after its death.

> "Speak unto Aaron and to his sons, saying, This is the law of the sin offering: In the place where the burnt offering is killed shall the sin offering be killed before the LORD: *it is most holy*. The priest that offereth it for sin shall eat it: *in the holy place* shall it be eaten, in the court of the tabernacle of the congregation. Whatsoever shall touch the flesh thereof *shall be holy*: and when there is sprinkled of the blood thereof upon any garment, thou shalt wash that whereon it was sprinkled *in the holy place*" (Leviticus 6:25-27).

The fourth chapter of Leviticus teaches that regardless of a person's temple standing (whether priest or common person) the sin offering had to meet the same qualifications: WITHOUT BLEMISH (verse 3, 28; also 9:3). Peter tells us that Christ fulfilled these requirements when He offered Himself "as a lamb *without blemish* and *without spot*" (1 Peter 1:19). He "offered Himself without *spot* to God" (Hebrews 9:14).

The apparent truth from the levitical ritual is: the sin-offering had to be without defect to symbolize a perfect Savior being offering for the sins of the world. It had to be guiltless itself in order to bear the guilt of the people. At no point did the sin offering become unholy. The sin offering was MOST HOLY, had to be eaten in A HOLY PLACE, and anyone who touched it became HOLY.

The law of the trespass offering was the same: *it is most holy* (Leviticus 7:1). Once again the same Hebrew word means either "trespass" or "trespass offering" depending on how it is used in the text. The word is *'asham* and is a reference to something most holy when used for "trespass offering" and something wrong when used for "trespass." *(Wilson's Old Testament Word Studies* gives a lot of interesting information.)* Isaiah used *'asham* in 53:10 when he said the Messiah would be an offering for trespass. This does not mean Messiah would be a trespass but a trespass offering.

In 2 Corinthians 5:21 the Greek word for "sin" is *hamartia* which is used repeatedly throughout the New Testament for "sin." Because of this, some stop their investigation and say Jesus was made into sin itself. The Jewish teachers would not have made this mistake. Two hundreds years before the birth of Christ the Hebrew Old Testament was translated into the near universal Greek language of the day by seventy ancient rabbinical authorities. When working on what is now known as *The Septuagint* (or LXX abbreviated), these Hebrew scholars used the same Greek word Paul used in 2 Corinthians 5:21 *(hamartia)!* They used *hamartia* in translation of the Hebrew words *chatta't* and *'asham*. No doubt Paul likewise used the word in 2 Corinthians 5:21.

Moses, Jesus, and Paul all taught that "out of the mouths of two or three witnesses" every word is established. There is only one witness in the entire New Testament that says Jesus was made sin (which as we have seen was a Hebraism for the sin offering). Note that Peter taught the believers of his day who were suffering persecution for doing good that Christ was likewise righteous when He suffered for sin: "For it is better, if the will of God be so, that ye *suffer for well doing*, than for evil doing. For Christ *also* hath once suffered for sins, the just for the unjust..." (1 Peter 3:17-18). John acknowledged as we must also that in the eternal Son of God "IS NO SIN" (1 John 3:5).

Consequently, because Jesus did not die as a sinner, but as a substitute for sinners, He remained holy (like the levitical sin offerings) BEFORE, DURING, AND AFTER His crucifixion. Today He is to be "eaten in a holy place" as we partake of Him in faith making us holy when we touch Him! Praise God!

Jesus was offered *for* sinners, not *with* them. "But God commendeth His love toward us, in that while we were yet sinners, Christ died FOR us" (Romans 5:8).

Brother So-and-So says Jesus spoiled principalities and powers in hell. Isn't he right?

Not if he says Jesus spoiled principalities and powers *in hell.* The Word says He did it on the cross! Note the complete statements of Colossians 2:14-15:

> "Blotting out the handwriting of ordinances that was against us, which was contrary to us, and took it out of the way, nailing it to HIS CROSS; And having spoiled principalities and powers, He made a shew of them openly, triumphing over them IN IT."

"[God] disarmed the principalities and powers ranged against us and made a bold
display and public example of them, in
triumphing over them in Him and in it [the
cross]" *(Ampl.)*

Many translators give a footnote that "the
cross" is an alternate rendering of "in it."
Clearly it is a gross mistake to interpret "in it"
as meaning "in hell." A few authorities even
render the pronoun with gender "in Him"
referring to God's triumph over principalities
in Christ.

Doesn't First Peter 3:18 teach that Jesus was made alive in the spirit proving He died twice—physically and spiritually?

Before I answer the first part of your
question, allow me to address the last part of
your inquiry. It has been often said that Jesus
died twice. In Isaiah 53 the original says
"deaths" in reference to the Messiah. Of course
Isaiah (as well as the other Old Testament
writers) also said "Lords" when he meant
"Lord" and "Gods" when he meant "God." The
Hebrew language, as the primers tell you, uses
the plural of a word to emphasize the importance of a thing, event, person, etc. If one is
especially good looking, a Hebrew admirer
might tell her she has "faces."

Not knowing the above simple facts about the Hebrew laguange has led many preachers to err about Christ's "deaths," saying this meant he died twice. In contrary view, Isaiah was teaching that His death would be extremely important.

Paul spoke of a singular death in Philippians: "Even *the* death of the cross" (2:8). He stressed a single death to the Romans also: "...when He died for sin, He died once..." (6:10, *Beck).* Christ died one time.

The New Testament makes it clear that Christ died ONCE, which proves again He didn't go to gehenna which in its expanded state will be known as the *second death.* Please compare the following two verses:

"For in that He died, He died unto sin *once...*" (Romans 6:10.

"And death and hell were cast into the lake of fire. This is the *second* death" (Revelation 20:14).

In answer to the first part of your question, 1 Peter actually teaches that Christ remained alive spiritually when He was put to death physically so that He could preach to captive spirits. Fenton translates the Greek of this verse correctly which ties it beautifully with verse 19: "Because even Christ once suffered for sinners, the Just for the unjust, so that He might bring you to God; *having been physically put to death, but spiritually living;* in that condition He also went and preached to the spirits under guard who were formerly apathetic, when the patience of God was waiting in the time of Noah..."

Doesn't Philippians 2:5f teach that Jesus laid aside His divinity when He became a man so that He could die as a man—both physically and spiritually?

The *kenosis* or "self-emptying" of Christ does not mean that Jesus emptied Himself of His divine nature at the Incarnation (or "emptied Himself of Himself" as the phrase is sometimes worded). It does mean He emptied Himself of His outward form as God and was made in the outward form as man. He laid "aside His desire to be worshipped, the legitimate desire of deity, in order to come to earth, take upon Himself the outward expression of a bondslave, and go to the cross for guilty sinners..." (Kenneth S. Wuest, *Word Studies from the New Testament*).

The clause "Who being in the form of God" (verse 6) has led some to mistakenly interpret that at the Incarnation He lost that form when He was "found in the form of man" (verse 8). The word "form" is rendered "outward expression" in the *Wuest Translation of the New Testament:*

"Let this mind be in you which was also in Christ Jesus, who subsisting permanently in that state of being in which He gives outward expression of the essence of deity, that outward expression coming from and being TRULY REPRESENTATIVE OF HIS INNER BEING, did not consider it a prize to be clutched, the being on an equality with deity (in the expression of the divine essence), but emptied Himself, having taken *the outward expression of a bondslave*, that expression coming from and being truly representative of His inner being, having become in the likeness of man. And having been *found in outward guise as man*, He humbled Himself, having become obedient to the extent of death, even such a death as that upon a cross..." (Philippians 2:5-8).

The outward form of the eternal Logos had to be changed in order to die. Jesus had to become a man in order to die, inasmuch as God cannot die, His inner being, however, remains eternally unchanged and did not die. We covered this point in the previous question and will not repeat it here. We will point out, however, another fundamental error of this teaching: it changes the unchangeable God. God cannot change and be God. "The Word was God Himself" (John 1:1, *Ampl.*). Had the inner being of Christ been made into sin and consequently died, then God was not in Christ when He reconciled the world unto Himself, but He says He was, so let's leave it at that.

Furthermore, Paul confirms the view that the two natures of deity and humanity perfectly resided in the Person of Jesus Christ. "In Him dwelleth all the fullness of the Godhead *bodily*" (Colossians 2:9). The divinity of Christ never died, but went to the Father at the death of the humanity of Christ.

The Epistle to the Hebrews also affirms the eternal unchanging character of Jesus Christ as never being altered in any way. A verse a lot of people *think* they know confirms this truth: "Jesus Christ the same yesterday, and today, and forever" (13:8). The Amplified says "is always the same." Clearly the inspired writer did not mean the outward form of Christ to be incapable of change (He wasn't a baby very long!). What he is obviously saying is the nature, character, and being of Jesus Christ—the eternal Logos (God)—is forever the same. He has not altered the slightest degree for all ages of ages—past, present, or future. (Note the difference in the outward form of the risen Lord in Luke 24, for example, compared with the glorified Lord of Revelation 1. During the 40-day interval between the resurrection and the ascension He both revealed and disguised Himself; passed through matter and yet was touched and felt. Yet He, the Logos, is the same and His years fail not.)

His inner being is the same today as He was yesterday when He was crucified and will exist forevermore without alteration. He is eternally immutable.

My pastor says that Jesus was a stench in God's nostrils at Calvary. What do you think about that?

Concerning the aroma of Christ on the cross, the Word says the opposite of your pastor. "...Christ loved us and gave Himself up for us as A FRAGRANT OFFERING and SACRIFICE to GOD" (Ephesians 5:2, *NIV*). "...Christ also loved you, and delivered Himself for your sakes as A SWEET PERFUME, an offering and sacrifice to God" *(Fenton)*. "...an offering and a sacrifice to God as a fragrant aroma" *(NASB)*. "...an offering and a sacrifice whose fragrance is pleasing to God" *(NEB)*.

This corresponds beautifully with the whole burnt offering of the old covenant which gave forth "the smell of a sweet savor" unto God (Genesis 8:21; Exodus 29:18, 25). The author of Hebrews compares the burning of the sacrificial animals to the physical suffering of Jesus outside the gates of Jerusalem: "For when the blood of animals is brought into the sanctuary by the high priest as a sacrifice for

67

sin, the victims' bodies are burned outside the [city's] gate in order that He might purify and consecrate the people through [the shedding of] His own blood, and set them apart as holy for God" (Hebrews 13:11-12, *Amplified Bible)*. The physical sufferings of Jesus outside the city limits of Jerusalem at Golgotha correspond perfectly to the burning of the animals' bodies on the Day of Atonement (Leviticus 16:27). This is why He said, "I THIRST'" (John 19:28). Jesus truly suffered for us—IN THE FLESH (1 Peter 4:1). The Greek word for "burnt offerings" in Hebrews 10:6,8 is *holokautoma,* from which we get our English word "holocaust." The word literally means "a whole burnt offering and is applied in the Bible to "a victim, the whole of which is burned" *(Thayer's Greek-English Lexicon).*

Jesus became our "holocaust" (whole burnt offering) outside the gates of Jerusalem at Golgotha, not in the fire of gehenna. "...the bodies are burned outside the camp. And so Jesus also suffered outside the city gate to make His people holy through His own blood" (Hebrews 13:11-12,*NIV).*

Concerning your pastor, I'll be praying for him...(and for evangelists and teachers, too).

What does the Bible mean when it says Jesus is the firstborn of the dead?

It does not mean that Christ was the first person to be reborn from spiritual death. Before answering this question specifically, there is the need to study "the firstborn" with all its various implications.

First, it must be understood that this designation of Jesus as "the firstborn" carries with it important doctrinal implications. In going back to the Old Testament where the term originated we see that the oldest son (the firstborn) in a Hebrew family had special precedence over ALL other sons. Jacob's sons were amazed at a feast prepared for them in Egypt by their long-estranged brother, Joseph. The unrecognized host surprised them all when he sat them in proper Hebrew order— the oldest to the youngest (see Genesis 43:33). The firstborn also received a double portion of his father's possessions (see Deuteronomy 21:16-17).

In like manner Jesus is "the firstborn among many brethren" (Romans 8:29). God promised, "I will make Him My firstborn, *higher than the kings of the earth*" (Psalm 89:27). Contrast this with Revelation 1:5: "And from Jesus Christ...the firstborn of the dead, and the *ruler of the kings of the earth*" *(NASB)*. It should also be understood that while believers are designated as "kings and priests" in the very next verse (Revelation 1:6), nowhere is any believer called "the firstborn." Thank God we are members of "the Church of the first-born" (Hebrews 12:23) which is another way of saying "the Church of Jesus Christ," since He alone is "the firstborn."

Second, the firstborn knew a special sacredness to Yahweh under Israel's covenant. The firstborn "both of man and beast" was set apart to God. "The firstborn of your sons you shall give to Me" (Exodus 13:2; 22:29).

In commemoration of Israel's deliverance from Egyptian bondage God said, "For all the firstborn are Mine; on the day that I struck down all the firstborn in the land of Egypt, I sanctified to Myself all the firstborn in Israel, from man to beast. They shall be Mine, I am the LORD" (Numbers 3:13, *NASB*). In fact, He took the tribe of Levi as the firstborn tribe. "So the Levites shall be Mine" (Numbers 3:12) and from that point on the Levites devoted themselves to the sacrificial system. In like comparison Jesus was wholly dedicated to the will of His Father. "For I came down from heaven, not to do Mine own will, but the will of Him that sent Me" (John 6:38). "My meat is...to finish His work" (John 4:34).

Third, Jesus is "the firstborn of all creation" (Colossians 1:15). Not in the sense of time, since the uncreated Christ effected the creation, but, in the sense of deserving the highest position of all the creation. "His is the primacy over all created things" *(NEB)*. This shows us His supremacy over all creation in the highest place of honor. The two Greek words used in the New Testament for "firstborn" are *primogenitus* and *protekos*. The former word means basically "first son" and the latter refers to "first fruit" *(primo* = first, primary, chief — *genitus* = offspring, son — *pro* = first, before — *tekos* = fruit, birthed. "Tekos" comes from *teko* which means "root." The word *protekos* is the parent word of "produce" which signifies the best of the crop).

Thus we see that Jesus as "the firstborn" (or "first begotten" in old English) is the best of the crop of sons God is bringing forth to glory (see Hebrews 2:10). He is the supreme Son in contrast with all other sons. He is likewise the "firstfruits" (1 Corinthians 15:20) since He was "the grain of wheat that fell into the ground and died" bringing forth "much fruit" (John 12:24). In this picture He is "the firstfruits of the harvest of the dead" *(NEB)* which means Jesus was the first Son God ever fathered. This brings us to the point of asking, "Exactly when did Jesus become the firstborn?" To which the Bible answers, "And again, when *He bringeth in the first begotten into the world,* He saith, And let all the angels of God worship Him" (Hebrews 1:6). The angels obeyed as recorded in Luke 2:13, "And suddenly there was with the angel a multitude of the heavenly host praising God..." Jesus became the firstborn Son when a virgin conceived by the Holy Spirit and "brought forth her firstborn Son and laid Him in a manger" (Luke 2:7).

Fourth, we can now understand better how Jesus, God's Firstborn Son is "the firstborn from the dead" (Colossians 1:18). He is the first Person raised from the dead who was birthed into a state of being (as a glorified King). The word "begotten" used in Hebrews 1:5 (see also Acts 13:33), quoted from the second Psalm is *gennao* which often denotes a literal birth, but which is also used "in a Jewish sense, of *one who brings others over* to his way of life in which God formally showed Him to be the Messiah by the resurrection" *(Thayer's Greek-English Lexicon).* "This day have I begotten Thee" and "the firstborn of the dead" are to be used Hebraistically or in the figurative Jewish sense of one's being introduced to a new way of life.

Christ's glory with the Father before the world was as the pre-incarnate Logos. Never before the ascension had a *man* sat at the right of God. Jesus, upon His resurrection from the dead, was birthed into a new realm of glory. This realm also belongs to those who fall alseep in Him. Paul termed Christ as "the firstfruits of those who have fallen asleep."

Like the firstfruits (Jesus), those who have fallen asleep with their hope in His appearing, will be raised PHYSICALLY (not spiritually as they are already raised with Him in that sense) FROM THE DEAD. They will experience the power of His resurrection in their lifeless bodies as mortality puts on immortality (see Romans 8:11). (Those who were raised from the dead prior to the resurrection of Christ were not positioned in glory in the heavens.)

Many discount His physical resurrection as the fulfillment of "the firstfruits" since others, such as Lazarus, had previously been raised. But there could be no stronger commentary on this than Paul's own words in Acts 26:23. "That Christ should suffer, and that He should be *the first that should rise from the dead...*" Others had been raised from the dead to die again, but "Christ being raised from the dead dieth no more" (Romans 6:9).

In conclusion, Jesus was the firstborn initially through a PHYSICAL BIRTH out of a virgin's womb (in this sense He was born of the Holy Spirit), and the firstborn from the dead by a PHYSICAL RESURRECTION out of a rich man's tomb. "God hath fulfilled the same unto us their children, *in that He hath raised up Jesus again;* as it is also written in the second Psalm, Thou art My Son, *this day have I begotten Thee"* (Acts 13:33). A birth signifies a beginning which Christ experienced in becoming one of us and in the changing of His physical body into a new realm of glory. His spiritual being is the Eternal God and was never born.

In commenting on His physical birth the profound preacher of the former century, William S. Plumer, said in his commentary on Hebrews (first published in 1872): "Divinity cannot suffer. Divinity cannot die. The divine nature of the Son is as incapable of suffering as the divine nature of the Father or of the Spirit. It never did suffer. It was the human nature that submitted to the curse of the law. One great design of the Incarnation was that the Redeemer might have a nature capable of suffering and dying—a nature that could be made an offering and a sacrifice to God."

Spurious Statements and Why

In this chapter we will look at various statements made by various preachers and teachers. There is no need to name the book, tape, or individual making each statement as we are not attacking ministries (many of whom are quite sincere, but misinformed), but exposing erroneous and spurious (counterfeit; false) teaching. This error is not confined to one group, as many suppose, but is found in three different persuasions of the full gospel belief and in one specific camp of evangelical fundamentalism.

The Apostles' Creed teaches Jesus descended into hell.

If, by this statement, one means that Jesus descended into hades (which is often translated "hell"), we would certainly agree for reasons already explained in this book. However, this phrase itself is not in the oldest records.

The Apostles' Creed, says Justice Bailey in his 1813 book *Common Prayer*, is "not to be understood that this Creed was framed by the

Apostles, or indeed that it existed as a Creed in their time..." (page 9). In fact, the phrase "He descended into hell" was not in the Apostle's Creed before the year 600 A.D.

Archbishop Wake says, "The most important 'addition,' since the year of Christ 600, is that which affirms, that Christ *descended into hell.*" This has been proved not only to have been an *invention after the Apostle's time,* but even after the time of Eusebius. Bishop Pearson says (in *Pearson on the Creed,* 1676, p. 225) that the descent into hell was *not in the ancient creeds* or rules of faith. "It is not to be found in the rules of faith delivered by Irenaeus, by Origen, or by Tertullian. *It is not expressed in those creeds which were made by the councils as larger explications of the Apostles' Creed; not in* the Nicene, or Constantinopolitan; *not in* those of Ephesus, or Chalcedon; *not in* those confessions made at Sardica, Antioch, Selucia, Sirmium, etc...It is *not in* the creed expounded by St. Augustine." (See *The Lost Books of the Bible,* p. 92, for this and more information.)

Furthermore, the supposed antiquous book of *Nicodemus,* also known as *The Acts of Pontius Pilate,* (which appears to be the work of a misguided monk) stresses four chapters that Christ descended into hell to defeat Satan and loose those appointed unto death. Whoever wrote this spurious gospel, which has been soundly rejected by all councils, claimed that the crucified Christ descended into hell at which time He defeated Satan and placed him under the dominion of Beelzebub! At that time Jesus loosed *all* souls (righteous and unrighteous) and carried them to heaven. This man had an imagination that would put the most elaborate war-in-hell storytellers to shame. I will quote from this spurious work only to illustrate my point:

"David replied to the prince of hell, and said, I understand the words of that vice... And now, thou filthy and stinking prince of hell, open thy gates, that the King of Glory may enter in...Impious Death and her cruel officers hearing these things were seized with fear...who art Thou, who with such courage enterest among our abodes, and art not only not afraid to threaten us with the greatest punishments, but also endeavourest to rescue all others from the chains in which we hold them?...Then the King of Glory trampling upon death, seized the prince of hell, deprived him of all his power, and took our earthly father Adam with Him to His glory...Then the prince of hell took Satan and with great indignation said to him, O thou prince of destruction, author of Beelzebub's defeat and banishment...O Satan, thou prince of all the wicked...now there is not one of them does ever groan, nor is there the least appearance of a tear in any of their faces. O prince Satan, thou great keeper of the infernal regions, all thy advantages which thou didst acquire by the forbidden tree, and the loss of Paradise, thou has now lost by the wood of the cross...Why didst thou venture without either reason or justice, to crucify Him, and hast brought down to our regions a person innocent and righteous, and thereby hast lost all the sinners, impious and unrighteous persons in the whole world? While the prince of hell was thus speaking to Satan, the King of Glory said to Beelzebub, the prince of hell, Satan, the prince shall be subject to thy dominion for ever, in the room of Adam and his righteous sons who are Mine" (taken directly from the supposed book of *Nicodemus*, chapter 15-18). [1]

In refutation of this concoction one need only notice a few discrepancies from the Word of God at a surface glance: Beelzebub (who in actual fact is Satan) being made lord over Satan rather than Christ; all the impious and unrighteous souls already in hell are delivered from eternal damnation; Satan said to be the keeper of the infernal regions (which we have clearly shown in this book to be a fairytale), etc. *ad nauseum.* Those who say that Jesus defeated Satan in hell and cut in twain the

[1]The quotation from *Nicodemus* taken from *The Lost Books of the Bible* reprinted in 1979 by Bell Publishing Company. This book is a compilation of spurious writings over which there has been unanimous agreements by evangelical scholars of their uncanonical nature.

iron bars of gehenna in our day can look back to this product of the dark ages for further confirmation of their message! (I apologize to those of you who will dislike my using that above quotation from a spurious writing, but it serves well to illustrate the point.)

When Jesus conquered Satan He unlocked the gates of hell and let the captives go free.

The "captivity" (Ephesians 4:8) which Jesus led in His ascensional train were not those formerly in gehenna. Know this: (1) under the Law sin was not removed—Hebrews 10:4; (2) at His death Jesus made redemption for the transgressions under the first covenant—Hebrews 9:15; (3) Abraham, who was in charge of paradise, saw the Incarnation and rejoiced, knowing he would soon be in the city built by God for which he had left Ur of the Chaldees—Luke 16:22-31, John 8:56, Hebrews 11:10, 13, 16; (4) the righteous Israelites were gathered unto their people at death. To prove this does not solely mean the physical burial vicinity see Genesis 49:33 and 50:1. Jacob died "and was gathered unto his people" whereupon Joseph kissed his unburied face and instructed the embalmers to embalm his father. Jacob was gathered unto his people more than FORTY SEVEN DAYS before he was finally buried in the cave of Machpelah (Genesis 50:2-

13). (5) Jesus told the repentant thief he would be with Him *that day* in paradise—Luke 23:43; (6) Years later Paul said he (or perhaps someone else) was caught up into the third heaven into paradise—2 Corinthians 12:2, 4— proving paradise had been moved; (7) men are appointed unto death after which they are judged—Hebrews 9:27; (8) the Bible nowhere teaches that people will be released from gehenna once there—Luke 16:26 ["neither can they pass...from thence (hellfire)"].

This subversion of the Scripture is approaching the dangerous falsehood of ultimate reconciliation, which teaches people will only spend an age or two in the lake of fire being purged from their sins. It is most likely that King Saul went to gehenna; if so, he is still there.

The bulls of Bashan were large demons ready to seize Jesus on the cross and carry Him to hell.

The bulls of Bashan referred to in Psalm 22:12-13 were a symbol of the merciless religious leaders mocking the crucified Christ. I believe Dake was correct: "Bulls are emblems of brutal strength. They gore and trample down all before them. Bashan was a district east of Jordan where the largest and fattest cattle were raised. Strong bulls of Bashan symbolize the headstrong rulers of Israel determined to destroy the Messiah" *(Dake's Annotated Reference Bible,* note p, Psalm 22).

Furthermore, it is a wise policy to base typology on several occurrences in the Scriptures. Where are bulls symbolic of demons in the Bible? They are not tied with serpents, scorpions, flies, etc. They were used in making offerings to God in several places in the Old Testament which a demonic symbol could not fulfill.

In Luke 23:43 the comma should be placed after "today" rather than before it.

This is a point some cults also make. Out of the more than 100 translations of the New Testament only two or three translations do this. It is senseless to do this as the dying man knew what day it was in which Christ was speaking to him (his last)! Confronted with the obvious sillyness of this position one teacher has reversed his position in recent months. He now says that Christ did go to paradise the day He died where He dropped off the repentant thief before proceeding on to gehenna. Two errors are obvious in the revised position: (1) The unrepentant thief must have accompanied Christ on down to gehenna. (2) The beggar was "carried *by the angels* into Abraham's bosom" (Luke 16:22) and Jesus was supposedly in the clutches of Satan. The Bible infers the devil could not go there.

The former position itself contradicted the Word of God. If Jesus did go to gehenna He could not have passed over into paradise later. Notice the words of Christ quoting Abraham's response to the lost man: "And beside all this, between us and you there is a great gulf fixed: so that they which would pass from hence to you cannot; neither can they pass to us, that would come from thence" (Luke 16:26).

Had Jesus become the loathsome rag these ministers say He had become, I sincerely doubt whether Abraham would have recognized or welcomed Him. Many of these brethren do not recognize the great injustice they do to the Person of Jesus Christ. "Father, forgive them for they know not what they do."

Because Jesus was in the bottomless pit it is obvious He was in hell.

Romans 10:7 teaches that Christ was in the *abussos* which is translated "the deep" in that verse and as "the bottomless pit" in Revelation 20:3. Tying these two verses together, some teachers argue that Christ was surely in hell. They correctly point out that Christ was in the *abusso* while He was dead and Satan will be bound and thrown into the same place. What they fail to bring out is that the *abusso* is not hell fire. Please note Revelation 20:3, 10. In verse 3 the devil is thrown and sealed into the *abusso* for a one-thousand-year period. After this he is loosed for a little season during which he makes one final assault against the camp of the saints. Finally (and not before) he is "cast into the lake of fire" (verse 10). This occurs more than *one thousand years* after he was sealed in the abyss. As we have said all along, Christ surely did descend into the heart of the earth for three days and three nights. The righteous dead were kept in a special compartment there. They were in comfort, but likewise in confinement. They formed the "train" that followed the glorified King into the eternal city at His ascension. At that time the everlasting doors opened to welcome Him and His adorers into that holy city! "Lift up your heads, O ye gates; and be ye lift up, ye everlasting doors; and the King of glory shall come in. Who is this King of glory? The LORD strong and mighty, the LORD mighty in battle" (He spoiled principalities on the cross). "Lift up your heads, O ye gates; even lift them up, ye everlasting doors; and the King of glory shall come in. Who is this King of glory? The LORD of hosts (Yahweh-Sabaoth), He is the King of glory" (Psalm 24:7-10).

The gates, once opened, will nevermore be shut! "And the gates of it shall not be shut at all by day: for there shall be no night there" (Revelation 21:25).

Jesus won the keys of hell and death when He defeated Satan.

This is true, however, the battle ground should be noted as the cross, as shown in the previous chapter in commenting on Colossians 2:14-15, not gehenna where the devil has not yet been. In dying on the cross, our Lord destroyed "him that had the power of death, that is, the devil" (Hebrews 2:14). The present error teaches that Jesus snatched the keys out of Satan's hand in an imaginary war in the flames of hell. Literal keys should not be understood from the expression "the keys of death and hell (hades)" (Revelation 1:18) anymore than "keys of the kingdom" (Matthew 16:19) which were given to Peter.

These "keys" were actually awarded to Jesus by God as shown in Isaiah 22:22: "And the key of the house of David *will I lay* upon His shoulder; so He shall open, and none shall shut; and He shall shut, and none shall open." Compare this with Revelation 3:7, "these things saith He that is holy, He that is true, He that hath the key of David, He that openeth, and no man shutteth; and shutteth, and no man openeth..."

When Jesus was justified in the spirit He was made righteous once again.

What appears to have been an early church hymn or creed of faith is often cited as a proof text that Jesus was spiritually reborn. The phrase "justified in the Spirit" is interpreted as "made righteous in the spirit." The word for "justified" is the same in 1 Timothy 3:16 as used elsewhere in the New Testament. The meaning of the word *dikaioo* is not **to be made righteous,** but rather **to be declared righteous.** In this way "All the people that heard Him, and the publicans JUSTIFIED GOD..." (Luke 7:29). The people did not *make* God righteous, but *declared* (or vindicated) His righteousness in the answer Christ gave to John's disciples.

A person is made righteous in the act of regeneration. A person is declared righteous by the throne of God when he/she accepts the blood of Jesus. This is the sense in which "justified" is used in the Epistle to the Romans (Romans 5:1, 9).

Jesus was declared to be righteous by His physical resurrection. Note the NIV translation: "He appeared in a body, was *vindicated by the Spirit...*" Clearly we are not to understand this tremendous statement as meaning our Lord was regenerated in His spirit. The Holy Spirit vindicated Jesus by quickening His lifeless body: "...who through the Spirit of holiness was declared with power to be the Son of God by His resurrection from the dead: Jesus Christ our Lord" (Romans 1:4).

Through demonized frenzies of the angry mob Pilate delivered Jesus over to be crucified because he feared the people. The Holy Spirit reversed their decision and vindicated the righteousness of Jesus in the resurrection. It was foretold in the Psalms. "Thou hast delivered Me from the strivings of the people; and Thou hast made Me the head of the heathen: a people whom I have not known shall serve Me" (18:43).

Satan stirred up the crowd inciting mass hysteria in otherwise intelligent people. He wanted Jesus put to death so he could kill Him spiritually with its sting. He was fooled as God caught him in his own craftiness and put him to an open shame, thereby defeating him at the cross. Jesus yielded up His spirit to the Father and was not touched by the wicked one. Satan thought he could touch His spirit, but he could not. He now lies and says he did what he did not do. The hidden wisdom of God was never seen by the devil. Had he seen it he would not have been caught in his own trap. "Which none of the princes of this world knew: for had they known it, they would not have crucified the Lord of glory" (1 Corinthians 2:8). "He that diggeth a pit shall fall into it..." (Ecclesiastes 10:8).

As Jesus hung on the tree the sky above Him was darkened by multitudes of evil spirits.

"Now from the sixth hour there was darkness over all the land until the ninth hour" (Matthew 27:45; also Mark 15:33). We are not told in Matthew or Mark what caused the darkness. We are told specifically in Luke ruling out further speculation: "and it was about the sixth hour, and there was a darkness over all the earth until the ninth hour. AND THE SUN WAS DARKENED, and the veil of the temple was rent in the midst" (Luke 23:44-45).

That does make more sense, doesn't it? Demons are spiritual, not material, entities. That they could cause physical darkness is not evidenced. The spiritual darkness they bring is what we are partly exposing in this book.

The sun will be darkened again in the not-too-distant future. It will be a divine, rather than demonic, supernatural act. It is not any harder for our all-powerful God to turn off the sun than it is for us to turn off a light. God specifically says it is *He* who shows wonders in the sky above: "And it shall come to pass in the last days, *saith God...* *I* will show wonders in heaven above, and signs in the earth beneath; blood, and fire, and vapor of smoke: the sun shall be turned into darkness, and the moon into blood, before that great and notable day of the Lord come..." (Acts 2:17; 19-20). [This does not contradict with the beast calling fire down, etc., in order to purposely deceive men into believing he is God (Revelation 13:13-14).]

The "scapegoat" on the Day of Atonement symbolized Jesus bearing our sins to hell.

My friend, C.C. Grant, has some unique comments on the events of Yom Kippur and their several meanings.

"In the book *Billy Graham Speaks* there's a rich insight into the origin of the word *atonement*. Mr. Graham says, 'William Tyndale, who translated the New Testament into English, encountered difficulty in finding a word to convey the meaning of Christ's redeeming work. Finding no suitable word, he joined two simple words—*at* and *one-ment*, making *atonement*.'

"In Leviticus 16, the Day of Atonement was a type of the complete reconciliation of God and man through the substitutionary work of Jesus Christ. This is illustrated by two goats, one animal DYING as a sin offering, the other LIVING as a scapegoat.

"Because of sin, God could not look upon man. Because of guilt, man could not look upon God. The two goats represented what happened when AT-ONE-MENT was made.

"When the high priest sacrificed the first goat, its blood became a covering for sin so that God could approach man. The scapegoat signified the removal of guilt so man could approach God.

"With the scapegoat, the high priest did three things (Leviticus 16:20-26)...(1) He laid his hands upon its HEAD; (2) he made an open CONFESSION; (3) he released the goat ALIVE into the wilderness.

"In doing these three things, the high priest was expressing faith in the substitutionary sacrifice *which had already taken place in the temple*. The shedding of blood had already satisfied God's requirements, as PROVEN by the fact that the high priest had been permitted to enter the Holiest, beyond the veil (v. 15). Yet, reconciliation was not *appropriated* until CONFESSION took place. By placing his hands on the HEAD of the scapegoat, the high priest symbolized the 'erasing of memory' for another year (v. 34). This was the weakness of the old covenant, for 'in those sacrifices there is a *remembrance* again made of sins *every year*' (Hebrews 10:3). But in the new covenant established in Jesus' blood, God says: 'Their sins and their iniquities will I *remember no more*' (v. 17).

"When the high priest placed his hands on the head of the scapegoat and made his

CONFESSION, he was literally saying: 'IT IS FINISHED (for another year). The blood offering at the temple is enough. Because the blood has been applied, God can now look upon man. With the releasing of the scapegoat there is the removal of guilt so man can approach God. God and man are AT-ONE for another year!'

"This is a beautiful picture of what happened at the cross. In His Incarnation, Jesus was manifested *in the flesh* to satisfy the requirements of both God and man—making them AT-ONE through the offering of Himself.

"In John 2:19-21, Jesus referred to His BODY as the temple (where the sacrifice took place). As our Substitute, He 'bare our sins in His own BODY on the tree' (1 Peter 2:24), as the innocent for the guilty, paying sin's penalty so that God could look with favor upon us. Then Jesus gave CONFESSION that His death at the cross was enough by proclaiming 'IT IS FINISHED!' Then, as 'the High Priest of *our confession*' He released His LIVE spirit into the hands of the Father: 'Into Thy hands I commend My spirit' (Luke 23:46).

"When the Father accepted the spirit of Jesus from the cross, it was proof that what happened there was enough. Paul says that God was... 'Blotting out the handwriting of ordinances that was against us, which was contrary to us...*nailing it to His cross*' Colossians 2:14. When that happened, we know the devil's hold upon us was broken, for the next verse declares: 'And having spoiled principalities and powers, he made a shew of them openly, triumphing over them in IT (the cross)' —v.15.

"This is why Satan seeks to conceal the glory of the cross and rob us of this wonderful truth. It was at the crude and simple cross he was defeated once and for all. There, the innocent blood of Jesus availed for sin and His triumphant confession 'IT IS FINISHED' affirmed the removal of our guilt!

"In his ego, Satan resents the cross. He would have you believe that something more was required. But through the preaching of the cross, we intimidate the intimidator!"

In answer to your question, it's obvious from the above teaching that the scapegoat signified the "erasing of memory." This could not have been a type of Jesus bearing our sins to hell, for in Luke 16:25 the rich man in hell is told: "Son, REMEMBER..."

The literal blood itself could not atone.

Yesterday I was listening to a Christian cable network while dressing for a service. A "fundamental evangelical" was preaching on the subject of justification. He was stressing the various points Paul said we are, "...justified by _____ ." It was a fine message as he spoke on various phrases found in Romans: justified by grace, justified by faith, justified by God, etc. Then he came to 5:9 and said "We are justified by blood. I do *not* mean the literal blood that flowed down the cross and soaked the ground." He then jumped to "justified by works" in James. I sat down on the edge of my bed and prayed for this man. He only had two sentences on the blood in his entire message. Out of those two sentences only one was a correct statement. This minister never explained the incorrect statement ("...I do *not* mean the literal blood...").

Jesus Christ meant the literal blood at the last supper He ate with His disciples: "...the new covenant in My blood which is shed for you" (Luke 22:20). He referred to the blood that would soon pour out of His body. Nowhere in the New Testament does Paul or James or anyone else say anything different.

I have heard similar statements made by ministers who claim to be baptized in the Holy Spirit. Jesus said the Holy Spirit would guide us into all truth. The Spirit and the blood agree (see 1 John 5:6-8). I can testify before God that I have personally heard ministers say such errors in the various persuasions of the full gospel realm: classic pentecostal, neo-pentecostal, shepherding, sonship, and faith. Our High Priest must surely be praying for us: "Father, forgive them for they know not what they do."

I am praying for this book to reach the hands of many pastors, evangelists, and teachers. I am praying that its truths will reach their hearts. We are living in the perilous days Paul warned us of in 1 Timothy 4:1f. Some are departing from the faith by listening to the seducing spirits of error prevalent in the Church. The men who once preached the Word of God in its simple beauty are now preaching doctrines that demons teach.

God is gracious. Our Lord gave the Jezebel of Laodicea space to repent of her deeds. Brethren, let us repent and do the first works. Let us return to our first love. Judge what I say in the spirit in which it is said and realize I say these things for your profit. You have done much to honor and glorify Christ. You are dear brethren who err from the truth. Will you not cease from the vanities of your minds and cry out for mercy? Acknowledge the truth to the sheep and those who hear His voice will love you for it. We will give account for the things we teach and preach. Often I have needed the correction and exhortation of the brethren. "Let the righteous smite me in kindness. It shall be oil to my head. Let not my head refuse it." *God will shake those who persist in error after time is given for repentance.*

The Bible never says we are redeemed by anything *other* than the blood! Don't fight it—accept it—and heed Paul's admonition to the leaders of his day:

> "Wherefore I take you to record this day, that I am pure from the blood of all men. For I have not shunned to declare unto you all the counsel of God. *Take heed therefore unto yourselves*, and to all the flock, over the which the Holy Ghost hath made you overseers, to feed the church of God, which He hath *purchased with His own blood*" (Acts 20:26-28).

Our salvation is...
blood bought,
not
hell wrought.

"I have not written unto you because ye know not the truth, but because ye know it..." 1 John 2:21.

Deep inside each believer God has placed His great sensing device. His Spirit of Truth continually bears witness to what we read or hear, sifting out error and retaining the pure nutrients of God's Word that strengthen faith and help us grow and mature in Christ.

It is my conviction that the Holy Spirit will use this book as one of His "sifters" in the lives of God's people. It is written with the confidence that the Spirit of Truth will confirm its message to those who know truth.

You can minister to your brothers and sisters in Christ by sharing copies of this book with them. I am sending these out at cost as one of the outreaches of this ministry. We give away literally tons of printed material each year. Your donation is tax-deductible and will be used solely for this literature ministry. *THANK YOU!*

Clip and mail to: David Alsobrook Ministries
P.O. Box 2676
Paducah, Kentucky 42002

--- --- --- --- --- --- --- --- --- --- --- --- --- --- --- ---

Dear David,

Please send me _____ copies of "Was The Cross Enough" to pass out to other Christians. I am enclosing a gift of $_____ to cover costs and assist in your anointed literature outreach worldwide.

My Name _____

Address _____

City/ State/ Zip _____

About the Author

David Alsobrook is a living testimony to God's great grace. Although he was raised in a minister's home he rebelled against the church's teachings in his early teens. He became involved in all forms of sin embracing the hippy tradition of the late '60s.

Through active involvement in Transcendental Meditation a strong spirit of suicide obsessed his mind in the Summer and Fall of '69 until in his despair he called on the Name of the Lord Jesus Christ. He was born again on November 30, 1969, and read the Bible from cover to cover four times the first six months.

As a result of intensive study of the Word of God he was led into a conviction of the reality of the Baptism in the Holy Spirit for today. At the age of 17 he began traveling the country sharing the Gospel of Jesus Christ and teaching the Word of God without partiality to man's traditions.

God has confirmed His Word through supernatural signs and wonders on many occasions. David teaches the Kingdom of God on a wide variety of subjects. Dianne, his wife, assists him in ministering to people's needs. They are the happy parents of two lovely children and make their home in Paducah, Kentucky.